HERMANN, MISSOURI

A WALK THROUGH HISTORY

Dea Hoover

I0806701

REEDY PRESS

Dedication

Kay Schwinke is responsible for my original interest in, and later my affinity for, visiting Hermann. Her tireless efforts to encourage tour groups drew me to the town and kept me coming back. Luckily for me, her mentorship shaped my career, and her friendship has shaped my life.

On March 31, 2025, Mom passed away at home. Where she wanted. We were in final edits on the book. She wrote her own obituary to take that burden from me, and also to get it right. And I believe she did. She is missed. I keep trying to call or text her when something happens, or when I think of it. She is now with Dad, who would have been so proud of my becoming an author, and they can now watch things unfold together. I love you, Mom and Dad!

Reedy Press
PO Box 5131
St. Louis, MO 63139
reedypress.com

ISBN: 9781681064789

Printed in the United States

25 26 27 28 29 5 4 3 2 1

Table of Contents

Hermann in 1906
Courtesy of the
Library of Congress

Introduction

Walking clears my mind and soothes my soul. It slows my pace and allows me to take time to look and sense everything around me. What better way to see any community? When I am scouting areas for tours, I always walk the neighborhoods that are off the beaten path to really get a feel for a location and what sort of community it is. Hermann is especially inviting to pedestrians as the town was methodically laid out by the German Settlement Society of Philadelphia. I hope you find that space to relax, enjoy, and soak it all in during your exploration. And don't worry, adventure is part of the plan. We'll even go to the cemetery. It's one of the best stories.

I don't want to replicate here everything that can be found in the wonderful publications available from Historic Hermann, Inc. and the Gasconade County Historical Society. Many tomes have been written about the history of this German village. My intention is to offer fun walks that might pique your interest for delving into those more detailed works.

I strive to share with you facts that are interesting, to make suggestions I would give friends and folks on my tours, and, most of all, to give you the feeling of having immersed yourself in this Missouri small town unlike any other in the state.

Whether you are driving or coming in on the train, this book serves as a handy guide to get around town. I'm hopeful you will notice some things you might not have otherwise sought out. As you may know, my first book was a scavenger hunt, so I like to show people things they wouldn't normally think to observe.

The idea of walking these days is a funny thing. Articles pop up on my news feed talking about "silent walking." I was joking with a friend that I just call it *walking*, and he agreed! In my small Missouri hometown, walking to a specific destination was rarely done unless it was kids coming home from school. Mostly it's folks out for exercise. But truthfully, you can't walk for exercise in a small town; 15 people will stop to give you a ride because they think your car has broken down. Often, more visiting than walking winds up being accomplished, and that's another reason to love a small town and the folks who live there.

The passenger train line running smack-dab through the middle of Hermann is enticing, making the town very easy to visit, and harkens back to a bygone era. I enjoy riding the rails, relaxing or working, as the train carries me along places one cannot drive. Amtrak's Missouri River Runner now offers service twice per day to Hermann from Kansas City and St. Louis, including an extension of the Lincoln Line going all the way from Chicago to Kansas City. This convenience makes it very appealing to visit Hermann—no driving or parking! Deboard the train, and boom! You are at the cutest caboose you have ever seen, with a train station brimming with information about the area. Most days, you will find a volunteer awaiting your arrival to share the visitor's guide, answer any questions, and point you to the exceptionally clean restrooms inside.

If you're working on a family history connected with Hermann, I hope you can get a feel for this town and its people through these pictures and descriptions. While I was doing research at the

Aerial view of Market Street
Courtesy of Flying Squirrel Aerial Optics

Gasconade County Historical Society, it amazed me the amount of people researching genealogy from afar and having their questions answered by the volunteers. Because the community was initially planned by the German Settlement Society of Philadelphia, records were kept with amazing accuracy and continuity through the years, even before settlers set foot here.

On August 7, 1836, the town was organized in Philadelphia, Pennsylvania, and the first 17 settlers, including 8 children, arrived in the harsh winter of 1837. It was designed to be a place where German customs and cultures could be maintained, and it would be "a safe asylum for us, our children, and our descendants." The society purchased 11,300 acres here for $15,612, about $515,000 in 2025 dollars. This illustrates the enormous amount of faith the society had in its plan. The land agent, George Bayer, was taxed with many more duties than his title suggests and died in 1838. It has been speculated his death was due to the stress and his disappointment that he could not fulfill all the obligations the society requested. However, the settlers persevered, and by 1839 the town had grown to 450 residents.

George F. Bayer

"Hermann the German" is what I hear in my head when I roll into town and see Hermann the Conqueror staring at me with his sword. My grandfather's name was Herman. My mom's maiden name was Bontz, and she used it as her middle name. She always follows up by saying, "Now, isn't that a German name?" I grew up hearing that and not realizing what she really meant until I learned about German culture and traditions. Unbeknownst to me at the time, we practiced many of them in our home. It actually became clearer when I moved to St. Louis to attend Washington University. During my forays into the community, I learned about the German culture in the St. Louis region. Later, when I became a tour guide and a tour director, I really understood it: long names, everyone arriving 30 minutes early to be sure they are on time, and sometimes being a bit stoic until they warm up—and then it's all fun and games. Now that I have visited Germany multiple times, I notice a bit of that; however, the Germans are the biggest party around, and that makes for a fun time. I've started taking my customers to the Concert Hall and Barrel Tavern in Hermann because of its authenticity. It's almost like time travel and stepping into a bier hall in Germany. As one would expect, the food and especially the beer are great. I hire a local couple who have a polka band to play the accordion and sing. It's not more than one or two songs before everyone is clapping, singing along, and even dancing.

But why did I choose the town of Hermann for my second walking tour book? My husband and I were fortunate enough to start in Missouri Tourism when Kay Schwinke was heavily involved. We were blessed with her mentorship, enthusiasm, and knowledge about tourism and especially about Hermann. We would not be where we are without her. She really made me love tourism and this town, and I am forever grateful for her friendship and for the introduction to the most German town in Missouri.

Courtesy of the Library of Congress

The historical perspective in the book *Centenarians of Brick, Wood, and Stone* by Anna Kemper Hesse really clinched the deal for me. In the introduction, W. Phillip Cotton Jr. describes Hermann as ". . . a town of rich architecture and a strong and consistent 19th-century character." And my favorite part is his unequivocal statement that "The concentration of significant structures make the town as a whole much more important than those towns which have only a scattering of good buildings." I have to agree and that's another reason to visit Hermann.

The preservation has been made permanent with the 1972 National Register of Historic Places designation, and later a broadening of the district as described here: "Roughly bounded by Wharf, First, Mozart, Fifth, Schiller, Fourth, Gutenberg and Reserve Streets in Hermann, Gasconade County, Missouri."

By increasing the area, the risk of losing buildings has decreased and serves as a boundary for where preservation ends and modernity begins.

In addition to the efforts to create a historic district, Jim and Mary Dierberg decided 136 years after the settlers arrived that they wanted to invest in Hermann and preserve and share what the original German settlers created here. The Dierberg Educational Foundation's Hermann Farm is a great introduction to the roots of this German community, and it is worth a visit on your trip to Hermann.

I leave you with the closing remarks of the president of the Deutsche Ansiedelungs Gesellschaft zu Philadelphia (German Settlement Society of Philadelphia) in the Penn Hotel: "May our descendants have reason to bless the undertaking of their ancestors!"

I believe they have.

And now, let's have a walk around Hermann, the most German town in Missouri.

Now slip on your walking shoes and start treading those sidewalks and paths. Who knows? If you walk the paths of Hannibal and now Hermann, you may go on to join a volksmarch one day.

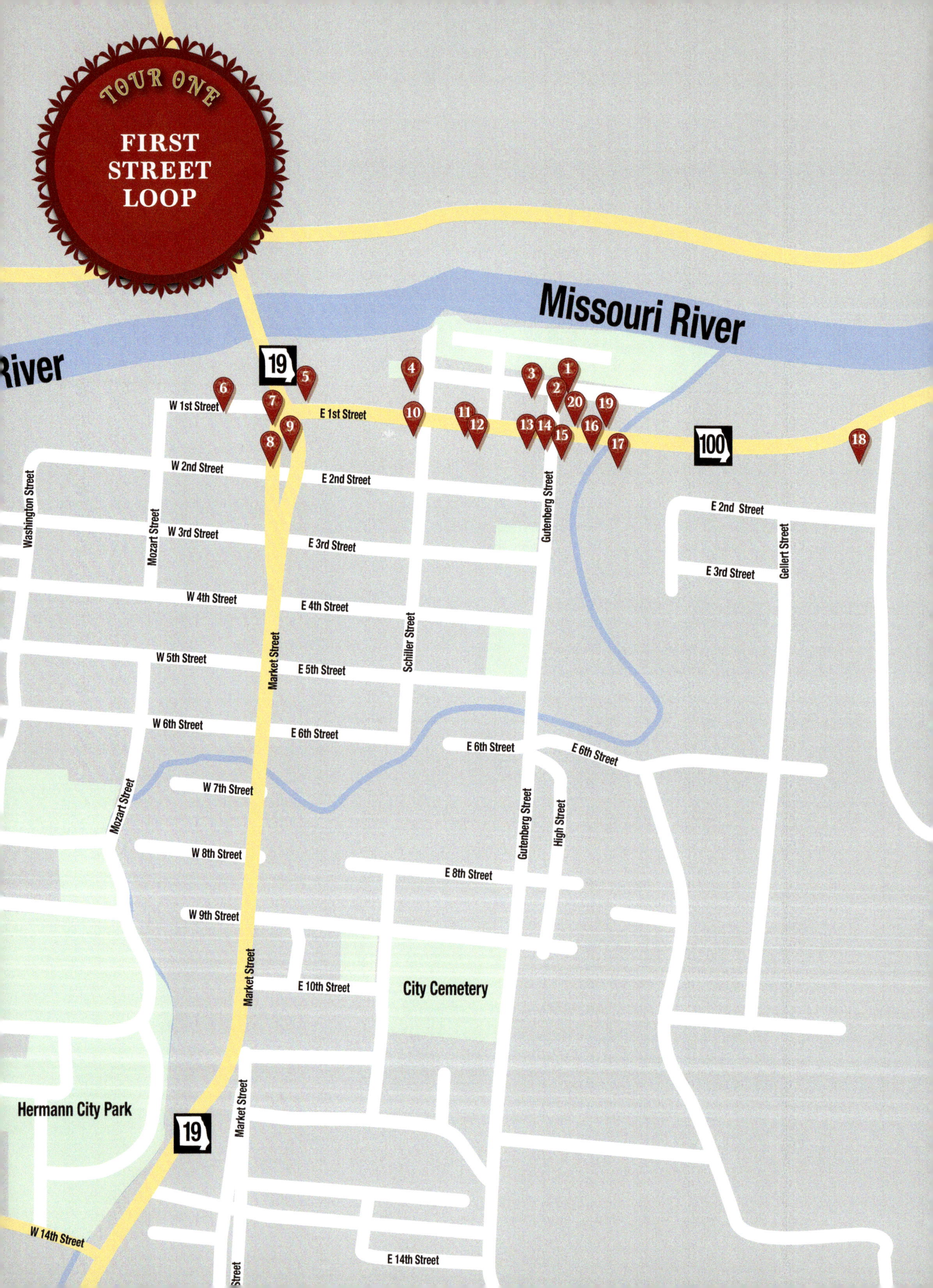

TOUR ONE
FIRST STREET LOOP
Missouri River
River
19
100
1
2
3
4
5
6
7
8
9
10
11
12
13
14
15
16
17
18
19
20
W 1st Street
E 1st Street
W 2nd Street
E 2nd Street
W 3rd Street
E 3rd Street
W 4th Street
E 4th Street
W 5th Street
E 5th Street
W 6th Street
E 6th Street
W 7th Street
W 8th Street
E 8th Street
W 9th Street
E 10th Street
W 14th Street
E 14th Street
Washington Street
Mozart Street
Market Street
Schiller Street
Gutenberg Street
High Street
Gellert Street
City Cemetery
Hermann City Park

TOUR 1
FIRST STREET LOOP

This walk, just slightly more than a mile, gives you a great first impression of Hermann. There are plenty of places for shopping, sipping, and savoring along the way.

If you arrive in Hermann by train, your walk begins as soon as you deboard. If you are driving, parking is available right by the red caboose. Begin your walk from there.

Courtesy of Flying Squirrel Aerial Optics

1 Hermann Visitor Information Center and Amtrak Station

301 Wharf St.
visithermann.com, amtrak.com

The first train passengers arrived in Hermann on August 6, 1855, in this same location. The journey through rolling hills and vineyards along the mighty Missouri River was exciting and new. They would have left the smoggy, soot-coated city of St. Louis and traveled aboard the Pacific Railroad.

Today visitors arrive on Amtrak, America's passenger train system. Two lines once stopped in Hermann: the Ann Rutledge that ran from Chicago to Kansas City, and the Missouri Mules (Kansas City Mule and St. Louis Mule) that ran between St. Louis and Kansas City. The Ann Rutledge line was a companion of the Abraham Lincoln line and was named after a woman from New Salem who may have been Lincoln's first love. The two lines were merged in 2009 to create the Missouri River Runner line. Hermann was only a seasonal stop, offering service during Maifest and Oktoberfest. With interest in the town increasing, Amtrak began offering regular service to Hermann in 1991. And since the Missouri River Runner line

Courtesy of Gasconade County Historical Society

offers twice-daily service to St. Louis and Kansas City, it is a fun and convenient way to visit Hermann for a day or for that weekend getaway at one of the many bed-and-breakfasts.

The new station opened in 2014 and features a stone veneer and traditional clapboard siding, with large windows to provide plenty of natural light. An important feature to many visitors is clean public restrooms inside! The building doubles as a Hermann tourist information center, and volunteers are there to greet almost every train's arrival.

2 Hermann Caboose Museum
301 E 1st St.

◆ As a labor of love, many volunteers have created this unique micromuseum. The Caboose Museum showcases life on the railroad in an authentic caboose. The caboose is where the rail workers would eat and sleep while not on duty, and the museum has been restored to its former glory, with historic artifacts such as an authentic caboose stove. Notice the lip around the edge of the top to keep anything being heated safe while the train rolled along. The stove also provided heat for the room in the winter.

The museum features a diorama that tells the story of the Gasconade Bridge Train Disaster. The Pacific Railroad was expanding westward, and Missouri Senator Thomas Hart Benton wanted the first transcontinental railroad to cross his state. A train full of dignitaries headed west to Jefferson City to celebrate the start of this transcontinental railway and encourage the government to support the project. The bridge across the Gasconade River was supported by temporary trestles, and although the engineer considered checking the bridge, he felt confident because a heavy train full of gravel had crossed it the day before. As they were behind schedule, they sent only one locomotive over to test the bridge before proceeding with the entire train. Unfortunately, the span collapsed, and the engine and seven cars fell through the bridge. Three other cars rolled down the hill toward the river, while only one car remained on the tracks. More than half of the 600 passengers were injured, and there were initially 31 known fatalities later revised to 43, including the engineer and dignitaries such as Henry Chouteau, a descendant of the founding family of St. Louis.

The most recent addition to the site is the train conductor statue offering a photo opportunity. Get out your camera and strike a pose!

Face the river and turn left (west) on Wharf Street.

3 White House Hotel
232 Wharf St.
thewhitehousehotel1868.com

◆ Don't be fooled by the name—the brick building with the blue doors and shutters is, in fact, the White House Hotel! From its founding in 1868,

Courtesy of Flying Squirrel Aerial Optics

Gottlieb Rippstein wanted his White House Hotel to be "one of the largest and finest hotels found on the Missouri Pacific Railroad Line." The hotel was named for railroad conductor Charles White, who managed the hotel and dining room for two unsuccessful years before returning the business to Rippstein. After a fire tore through the building in 1886, the hotel was rebuilt in the Victorian style before falling on hard times, with the ballroom at one time being converted into the Missouri Pacific Railway Dining Hall to feed the many military members heading out to training facilities before World War II. In 1971, Robert and Judith Plummer bought the hotel to save it from being converted into apartments, and they restored it to the Victorian era room by room for 50 years. The hotel offers incredible views of the river, especially from the Presidential Suite. It is also conveniently located near the train station, which enables guests to reach their accommodation easily, from rail or river. Guided tours are available to explore the many rooms, from ballrooms to barrooms—there's even a speakeasy from the Prohibition era.

Train by the White House Hotel
Courtesy of Gasconade County Historical Society

Continue west and turn left at Schiller St.

4 Fernweh Distilling Co.

4 Schiller St.
fernwehdistilling.com

◆ When it comes to walking tours, this local business has the best name, since in German *fernweh* would most commonly be translated as "wanderlust" (the literal translation is "far sickness"). It also connotes the desire to travel, or having itchy feet. The distilling company has both a tasting room and a restaurant with fantastic internationally inspired cuisine to fortify your body and your spirit. They own both the one-story and two-story buildings, so if you want a good photo of the sign, look up! The logo is a compass, and they will be happy to guide you through their various creations (if you are over 21, that is!). You will get an authentic local whiskey, as all spirits are distilled here in Missouri, and the master distiller is passionate about having quality water, quality grains, and carefully monitored distillation to provide the most perfect product.

5 Gasconade County Courthouse

119 E First St.

◆ You probably noticed this building while coming into town. Thanks to its copper roof, you can see it gleaming from miles away! This stunning municipal building was made possible by a $50,000 bequest from successful entrepreneur Charles Eitzen when he died, making it the only privately funded courthouse in the United States. Hailing from

Did You Know?

Brickmasons often brushed the bricks with vinegar to give them a uniform and shiny look. However, when the courthouse was built in 1896, they used beer, as it achieved the same look and was cheaper!

Courtesy of Gasconade County Historical Society

Did You Know?

The **original county** ran all the way from Franklin County to the Kansas border, then south from the Missouri River to present-day Licking.

Bremen, Germany, he found success in lumber and iron, originating the first Hermann ferry and then investing in Laclede Gas and several banks. He was mayor of the town and owned one of the first plots of land in 1837, when the German Settlement Society of Philadelphia portioned off its 11,300 acres.

Hermann was actually the fourth county seat, as the county was established before statehood. Interestingly, Daniel Morgan Boone, son of pioneer Daniel Boone, was the territorial commissioner at the time.

It is said that the name of the county was given to the area by the St. Louis French, most likely because of the fur traders and trappers who liked to regale people with their exploits and knowledge of the area. "Gascon" is the French word meaning "braggart," as those from the French province of Gascony were considered boastful.

Courtesy of Flying Squirrel Aerial Optics

6 St. Paul United Church of Christ

136 W First St.
hermannucc.com

Courtesy of Flying Squirrel Aerial Optics

❖ If you have driven into Hermann, you may have already seen St. Paul United Church of Christ, as its tall steeple rises up on the bluff overlooking the river. The congregation dates back to 1844, when the General German Church and the Evangelical Congregation of Hermann and the surrounding territory combined. The church provided almost 24 gallons of whiskey to the construction workers! They added onto the church on three different occasions. The first project was in 1893, when they built the bell tower and donated the old bell to the city of Hermann, which used it in their town hall. The second was in 1907, when they built the new church and bell tower—the stained glass was preserved and incorporated into the new build. The final project was in 1960, when they enlarged the church. Unfortunately, the parsonage and the church offices and educational building were destroyed by arson in 1990, but the congregation has pressed on and continued its mission to serve the community, with projects such as a food pantry and tutoring program for kids.

View of St. Paul United Church of Christ from Mozart Street
Courtesy of the Library of Congress

Did You Know?

Until 1925, **St. Paul United Church of Christ** had German-language services. As long as nine members or more in the congregation requested it, there would be a German service.

7 Hermann River Memorial
110 W First St.

◆ Attention, steamboat fans! This memorial is a full-scale model of the *John Heckmann*, the largest privately built steamboat on the Missouri River. The 9-foot pilot wheel is from the *John Heckmann*, built right here in Hermann, and narrative panels along the outside carry the names of Hermann rivermen.

Note: The pilot house is not open, but you can view it from the exterior.

Courtesy of Flying Squirrel Aerial Optics

Walk south on Market Street and turn right onto Second Street.

8 Deutschheim State Historic Site

101 W Second St.

mostateparks.com/park/deutschheim-state-historic-site

◆ You will see our next stop atop a small hill. A jewel of the Missouri State Parks collection, at the Deutschheim State Historic Site you can experience life as a new German settler in the 1800s. The word *Deutschheim* translates to "German home," and costumed interpreters will welcome you into the home, describing what life was like when Hermann was settled. The interpreters are present Thursday to Sunday, and reservations can be made for a group tour of 10 or more. Don't forget to see the Gemusegarten, or kitchen garden, located behind the preserved Pommer-Gentner House, built in 1840. Heirloom flowers and vegetables are planted in four squares, demonstrating how the original settlers would have planted both for their household use and to add beauty around their home. The four-square design created a walking path between areas, providing easy access for tending to the plants. The Brush and Palette Club saved the Pommer-Gentner House and were at the forefront of Hermann's historic preservation in the 1950s, and we have them to thank for this site that also includes the Strehly House (circa 1842), the Feldman-Stark House (circa 1883), and the Gentner Barn. They donated the buildings to Missouri in 1978.

Did You Know?

You can view a wine cask that is a smaller carved version of something akin to the **Apostle casks** that resided at Stone Hill prior to Prohibition. This one is 63 inches high, 43 1/2 inches across the end, and 57 inches long, constructed from oak wood staves with five metal bands. The front oval panel is carved with the figure of Bacchus, the Roman god of wine, celebration, and agriculture. He holds a bowl and lance, surrounded by grape vines. The inscription on the cask has the name of the winery where it resided: "PH Scheider & F Koeller, Hermann MO 1875." This cask was made for Franz Langendorfer for his natural cave wine cellar south of town. When Prohibition went into effect in 1920, most of the casks were destroyed or allowed to fall apart due to rot, termites, or woodworm. Be sure to check days of admission as the cask is inside. Guided tours are available.

Did You Know?

A program called **SPARKS** encourages bird-watching in Missouri through a partnership between **Missouri State Parks**, the **Department of Natural Resources**, and the **Missouri Birding Society**. Almost 80 percent of the 442 species of birds seen in Missouri have been spotted at the state parks. Learn more at sparks.mobirds.org.

Look east and walk across Market Street to the three flags around a statue.

9 Hermann: Germania's Liberator Statue

107 Market St.

◆ Next head toward the fierce protector standing in the plaza. Here stands the namesake of the town. Arminius, which is Hermann in the Germanic language, was the great Germanic leader of the Cherusci tribe who was the reason the Roman Empire stopped at the Rhine River. The Cherusci were allied with the Romans, and as the son of the chief, Arminius joined the Roman army, receiving an education and even citizenship and rising to the high rank of equite, similar to that of a knight. Shortly after his return to Germany he began to unite the tribes against the Romans, and he waited for the perfect moment to strike. When a massive rebellion broke out in the Balkan Peninsula, the bulk of the Roman forces in Germany were withdrawn, leaving only three legions. Arminius took advantage of this opportunity, bringing to General Varus reports of an uprising by the Germanic tribes north of them. Varus sent all the legions under his command northward, only for them to find themselves trapped along the narrow road, with the Cherusci and their allies attacking from the dense forest on either side of the track. All the Roman legions were annihilated, with some 20,000 casualties, making it one of the worst defeats suffered by Rome in its history, and it put an end to the Roman plan to conquer the region. Arminius continued to fight against the Romans until his death at age 25, when he was killed by his fellow tribesmen for becoming too powerful. Over time the name Arminius became linked with Hermann, particularly with Martin Luther, who drew parallels between the ancient story and the Lutherans of Germany standing up against the Roman Catholic church. Arminius became popular in literature and as a historical role model.

Continue east on First Street.

10 Espresso Laine

100 Schiller St.
espressolaine.com

◆ Head to the charming brick building with the white railing on the second-floor balcony that stretches across the entire front. Built in 1870–71, this was the Rudolf Schlender Residence and Commercial Building and now is the place to stop if you need a bit of a perk-up "where the locals hang out." Sure, wine might be the most popular reason for people to visit Hermann, but Espresso Laine is a fantastic hidden gem that has been voted best coffee shop in Missouri! Not only do they have amazing coffee, tea, and specialty drinks, they sell coffee beans in bulk with amazing flavors like Strudel Cake, Crème Brûlée, and Colombian Supremo. Pair these with the wonderful pastries like bacon cheddar scones, made from local ingredients. Their toy store, which proudly features nonelectronic toys, is sure to make parents and grandparents alike smile when picking out a gift. Sip and savor inside a building that is more than 150 years old.

Continue east on First Street. The next stop is on your right.

11 Concert Hall and Barrel Tavern

206 E First St.
concerthallandbarrel.com

◆ If you are looking for the oldest tavern west of the Mississippi, you are in the right place. The Concert Hall and Barrel Tavern has never closed since it was built in 1878 by John Pfautsch and Phillip Kuhn. The Barrel Tavern name may be self-explanatory, but as the painted sign suggests, it has a functioning concert hall upstairs that has hosted concerts, dances, lectures, and more. In 1881 a bowling alley was added to the building for more activities. It has since been removed, along with the garden that was added in 1886 where the First Bank now stands. Spend a bit of time to truly appreciate the camaraderie and community found here. You won't regret time spent soaking in the ambience and historic atmosphere of this beloved gathering place.

Continue down the block to Stomp'n Grounds Espresso Bar.

12 Stomp'n Grounds Espresso Bar

214 E First St.
stompngroundsespressobar.com

◆ What's that? Hermann has multiple espresso bars? Yes, it does! Head to the building with the green fish-scale siding on the third floor to find Stomp'n Grounds, which prides itself on its exceptional focus on quality. Owners Jamie and Beth Walker traveled throughout the country to observe what makes a successful café, making it a place not only to enjoy a cup of coffee but also to connect with others. Just as their neighbors at the wineries obsess about the right grapes and ingredients, the crew at Stomp'n Grounds obsesses about their coffee, from using the most advanced technology to filter the water and grind the beans to knowing the origin of their ingredients, as they say, "from seed to sale." They are just as focused on their community, hosting Jam Nights on Fridays for local musicians to share their talent. Looking for something to do after your walking tour? Their staff is passionate about their hometown and are always willing to tell you what they love to do around town!

Continue heading east to Wurst Haus.

13 Hermann Wurst Haus

234 E First St.
hermannwursthaus.com

◆ Their name might be the wurst, but they are the best! You can't think of German food without the sausage and kraut. This unassuming building, which was previously an auto parts store, has some of the best meat in town, as Wurstmeister Mike Sloan has won more awards than he has wall space to display them all. With more than 600 awards at all levels, from regional and state to national and even international awards, including 15 Best of Show honors and 29 international awards from the German Butchers' Association in Frankfurt, Germany, you know you are tasting the best! He still creates all 65 varieties of sausages and bratwursts, as well as his Champion House-Smoked Bacon, in house. The store also sells amazing Wurst Haus craft beers and sodas, as well as other great gifts and gourmet foods. You can have your purchases shipped to your door—they make amazing gifts! Or if you are in town and the store is closed, check out the sausage vending machines. You've never seen anything like them.

Courtesy of
Hermann Wurst Haus

Courtesy of Flying Squirrel Aerial Optics

14 Hermann Star Mills Sign
238 E First St.

◆ Hermann Star Mills was built by Henry Reitemeyer and Mattias Kochele in 1867, and it completely revolutionized the milling industry of Hermann thanks to its steam-powered grist mill. Suddenly they were able to process more grain than Reitemeyer's old water-powered grist mill, as the five millstones propelled by the 125-horsepower steam engine produced 160 barrels of flour a day. George Klinger bought the property in 1872 and had increased production to 240 barrels a day by the 1880s. The mill eventually fell on hard times and was home to a variety of businesses, including a cheese factory, a warehouse for furniture and for paint, and even a pencil factory, before eventually being converted into a machine shop. The once brightly painted sign faded over time, but when Oncken Machine Service purchased the building in 1981, they began to repair it. However, the sign was not completely repainted until 2020 due to the death of their sign painter in a tragic train accident.

Courtesy of the Library of Congress

Continue east and cross the street. Look for the powerful Black Shire horse head or the golden deer atop the gates.

15 Black Shire Distillery Tasting Room and Hofgarten

111 Gutenberg St.
blackshiredistillery.com

◆ In the 1840s, a small family farm was established in Hermann, and like many of the immigrants, the Rasche family set up a small still. The Black Shire Distillery is built on this foundation, literally and figuratively, as it carries on the tradition of distilling spirits with a focus on sustainability, using grains from local farmers and aging spirits in barrels made from Missouri white oak that are charred down the road. Even the name refers to the Black Shire horses that can still be found on the nearby farm, brought in by Jim and Mary Dierberg. In addition to having a degree in viticulture, distiller Derek LeRoy has fermentation in his blood, as his father, Paul LeRoy, is one of the most prominent winemakers in Hermann. Enjoy one of the many spirits, either straight or in an amazing cocktail, as you sit in the tasting room or on the patio at the Hofgarten, which evokes a feeling of the old horse stalls that would have been found in this German community (even if the fountain was imported from France!). The golden deer that greets you on the fence was designed by Hans Droog, a local artist who works in both sculpture and paint.

Continue east.

Courtesy of Flying Squirrel Aerial Optics

BLACK SHIRE
DISTILLERY

Courtesy of the Library of Congress

16 G. Husmann Wine Co.

302 E First St.
ghusmannwine.com

◆ Located right next door on the other side of the corner from Black Shire Distillery is the G. Husmann Wine Co. While most have heard of the two largest wineries in town, Stone Hill and Hermannhof, you might have overlooked this quaint wine tasting room. The name comes from George Husmann, the father of the Missouri grape industry who put our wines on the map. He was a tireless researcher and later a professor at University of Missouri at Columbia, and he published numerous works that helped save the grapes of Europe from a deadly blight. Two statues in Montpellier, France, represent the appreciation for those in the US who helped rescue the French winestock. Husmann was also a prominent figure in the Napa Valley grape industry due to the rootstock from his Sedalia, Missouri, nursery, which helped steel the California grape stock from the same phylloxera (initially thought to be lice) that had attacked the French vine roots in 1863. After the discovery of the cause, Missouri sent roots back to France that were brought to the US during the French settlement. The US roots were resistant to the disease while the French roots were not. So, if you like wines from Missouri or California because they are reminiscent of French wines, you have George to thank! As for the wines at the tasting room, they are the brainchild of Paul LeRoy, who has been making wine in Hermann for more than 40 years, blending the wines that Husmann influenced to create a profile like no other. The wines are all named after someone who impacted George's life, so a tasting here is like a walking tour of his life.

The French wine industry is literally built upon Missouri roots because of George's phylloxera-resistant root-stock coming to the rescue.

Courtesy of Hermann Wine Trail

17 Hermannhof Winery

330 E First St.
hermannhof.com

◆ The first thing you might notice upon seeing Hermannhof is that it is old. Not only the building but also the cellars built into the hillside are all featured on the National Register of Historic Places. The building began as a combination winery and brewery when it was completed in 1852, and the winery was a smaller aspect of the venture, as the beer was the moneymaker. However, by 1904 wine became the main export from Hermann, with more than 3 million gallons made every year! Hermannhof's cellars were used by local vintners to house their wines, but sadly this tradition ended when Prohibition forced the

Courtesy of Flying Squirrel Aerial Optics

destruction of the fields. After the repeal of the Volstead Act, the wine industry slowly returned to Hermann, and in 1974 Hermannhof was purchased by the Dierberg family. They have returned it to full capacity, with 15,000 cases of wine produced every year. The barrels come from France and from locally grown white oak and are aged in the many cellars under the building. The winery has won many prestigious awards, and it was the first winery to win the Brown–Forman trophy for Best New World White Wine.

Continue walking .2 miles east until you see the gold deer and the fountain. You will be at the entrance of the next stop.

18 Hermann Farm

526 E First St.
hermannfarm.org

◆ Seeing that the old ways of farming were being lost, Jim and Mary Dierberg made it their mission to restore and promote the history of Hermann

after Jim's first visit in 1971. They have preserved this farm to show how the early families of Hermann would have made a life for themselves. Buildings have been brought onto the property that are true to German settlers, and George Husmann's house showcases antique furniture crafted locally. They have brought in the Black Shire horse breed and offer tours of this working farm. Book a wagon ride to see the view from above, visit the cemetery on the hill, then visit the tasting room of the distillery. Be sure to check out the Reserve Cellars located in the former press house of George Husmann, where you can taste the Missouri/California blend wines created for their brand.

Cross the road and return west on First Street.

19 The Wohlt House

415 E First St.
thewohlthouse.com

◆ Another one of the wonderful homes on the National Register of Historic Places, The Wohlt House was built in 1884 as the residence of Hermann's first mayor, August Wohlt, and his wife, Caroline. August made his fortune in the steam ferry trade, carrying goods across both the Missouri and Gasconade Rivers. If you are looking for a place to stay in Hermann, the house has three wonderful guest rooms, as well as a formal parlor and dining room. There is also an amazing deck on the second floor.

Continue west on First Street.

20 Tin Mill Restaurant

315 E First St. #1115
tinmillsteakhouse.com

◆ It's impossible to miss this iconic-looking restaurant, as the building that Tin Mill calls home was used as a grain elevator and mill for most of its existence, producing White Pearl Flour and Lucky Hard Wheat Flour that were shipped out along the Union Pacific Railroad. It was then converted into a Missouri Farmers Association (MFA), a farm cooperative distribution center, which served the community until being converted into the wonderful restaurant and brewery it is today. See some of the original grain-processing equipment on display as you enjoy one of the amazing beers that the restaurant produces, including traditional recipes that follow the German purity law for beer. With 20 different beers on tap, it's certain to please the beer lover in your group! The food is amazing as well, which makes the Tin Mill a perfect place to grab a bite, with appetizers like pretzels to a full sit-down meal with entrées from a traditional German dish, veal schnitzel, to a mouthwatering prime rib. You can also experience a twist on tradition with the seafood spaetzle. My husband and I grew up with spaetzle made by our grandmothers, although I never knew the German word for the noodles until I became an adult. It's a must-order side for us.

I also recommend the potato pancakes. Every chef has their own variation of the recipe, and I do believe you will approve of this one.

Courtesy of Flying Squirrel Aerial Optics

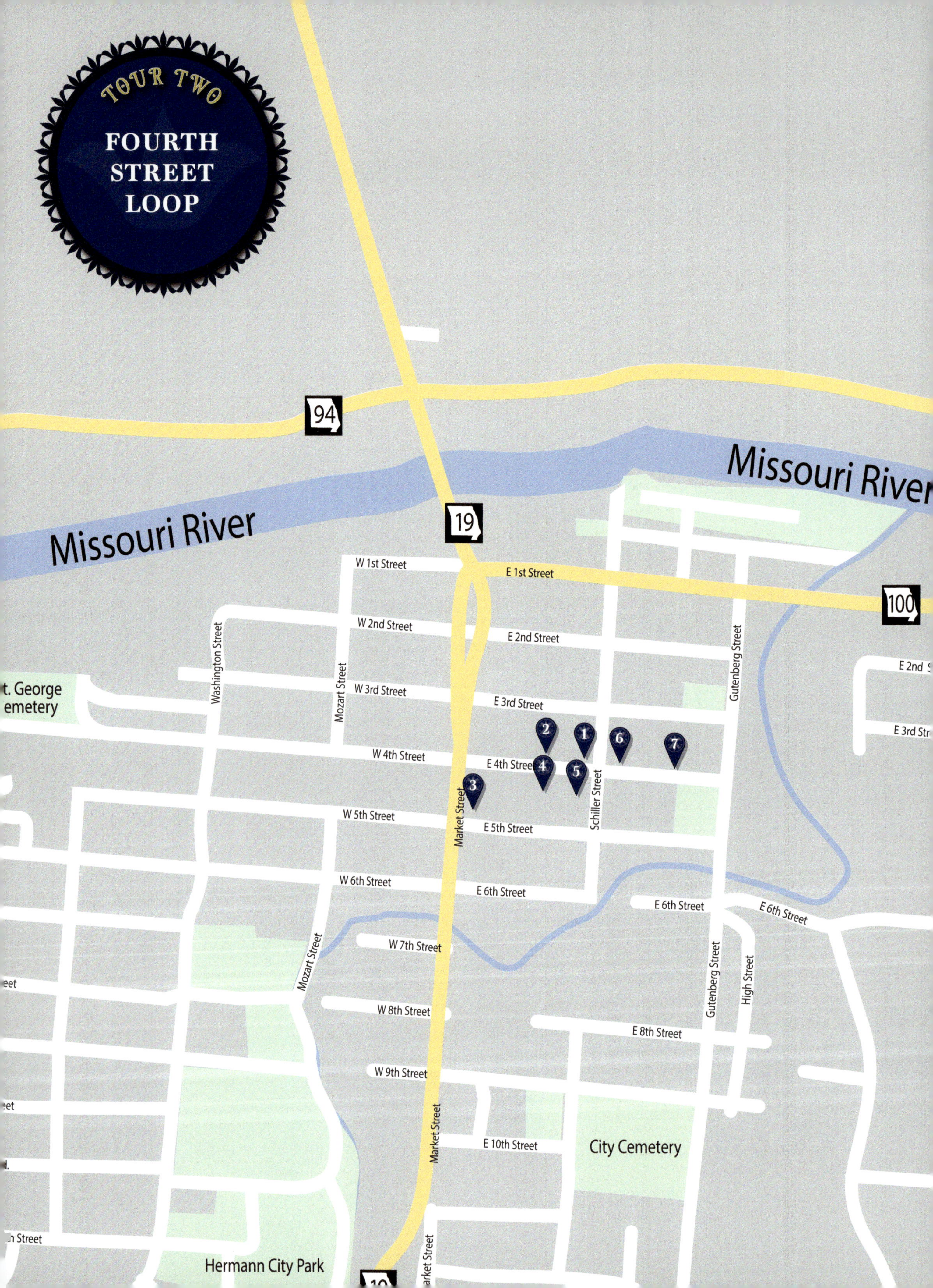

TOUR TWO
FOURTH STREET LOOP
94
Missouri River
Missouri River
19
100
W 1st Street
E 1st Street
W 2nd Street
E 2nd Street
E 2nd
W 3rd Street
E 3rd Street
E 3rd Str
W 4th Street
E 4th Street
W 5th Street
E 5th Street
W 6th Street
E 6th Street
E 6th Street
E 6th Street
W 7th Street
W 8th Street
E 8th Street
W 9th Street
E 10th Street
Washington Street
Mozart Street
Mozart Street
Market Street
Market Street
Schiller Street
Gutenberg Street
Gutenberg Street
High Street
t. George
emetery
City Cemetery
Hermann City Park
1
2
3
4
5
6
7

TOUR 2
FOURTH STREET LOOP

I've chosen this walk because it has lines of historic brick buildings on the National Register of Historic Places, and it bears noticing that this is not typical of many Midwestern towns. I've chosen a few places that are important, and others that are thriving in the area. There are other sites along the way, and you will find places to browse in and around them, including mini or pocket gardens.

1 Historic Hermann Museum
312 Schiller St.
historichermann.com

Located in the Old German School, Historic Hermann Inc. seeks to preserve the past for future generations to enjoy, especially artifacts relating to the town's unique German heritage. Historic Hermann was born at a public meeting on October 30, 1952. With the help of the National Trust, the organization was incorporated on January 1, 1953. Its charter calls for extending appreciation of the area's German heritage by providing a museum for receiving and preserving items of historic value. The

Did You Know?

German brides often wore black wedding dresses until likely the 1860s when Queen Victoria wore black for mourning. They were practical and could be used long after the wedding ceremony.

exterior feature it is known for is the clock tower. You may hear the bell in the tower ring when the clock hands move to the hour. Built in 1871, the Old German School was founded to teach classes using only the German language, and it did not close until 1955. The displays have been collected from residents over the years, and you will see interesting pieces such as a traditional black wedding dress, a dirndl dress, children's toys, and you might even be there when volunteers wind the clock in the tower every other day. You may see Corey Orr, president of Historic Hermann, dressed in a Union soldier uniform, sharing the story of the Civil War and its impact on Hermann's citizens.

Exit the museum. Turn right on Schiller. Turn right on Fourth Street.

❷ 4th Street Pizza

113 E Fourth St.
fourthstreetpizza.com

◆ Built in the late 1890s, this building is just one example of the many buildings along Fourth that have remained through the centuries. The building became a pizzeria in 2016. When Kathryn and Trigg Render moved to Missouri from the East Coast, the thing they missed most was the New York–style pizza they loved. (My husband is from New Jersey and can relate!) So, they started to make their own, first at home and then eventually right here on Fourth Street. I have to say, it makes me feel like I'm in a cozy pizza oven when I am inside, and it might feel that way for you too.

Continue west on Fourth Street. Turn left on Market Street. Go to middle of the block.

3 Sugar Momma's

411 Market St

sugarmommashermannmo.com

◆ Once upon a time in nearby Rhineland, a woman named Sylvia Bruckerhoff was known as the Pie Queen, and she would create amazing pies from scratch for everyone from friends and family to restaurants and churches. One year she made 600 pies! Baking is an important part of German heritage passed down through the generations. So, when Sylvia's daughter Tammy decided to open her own shop, who else would she name it after besides her Sugar Momma? It is located on the

widest street in town, and the variety of candies and gifts has been thoughtfully curated, including German and Amish candies and saltwater taffy. You can even order online and have a little bit of Hermann shipped to you.

Head north on Market Street and turn right on Fourth Street.

4 Showboat Community Theatre

112 E Fourth St.

showboathermann.org

◆ Built in 1934 by J. H. Helmers for owners Cap and Betty Bassman, 9-year-old Calvin Schermann won the naming contest with Her-Mo Theatre. He received a year's pass for his clever entry. In the 1970s it was renamed the Showboat by Jeff and

Courtesy of Visit Hermann

Janice Schmidt, who ran it for many years. Later, new owners were unable to continue the project, and First Bank acquired the building. In 1984 it was donated to the city of Hermann to be a community theater, and it has been run as a nonprofit ever since. The name reflects the excitement of showboats and riverboats visiting town and the importance of the industry to this community.

5 Topiaries

138 E Fourth St.

topigardens.com

◆ Opened as the *Hermann Volksblatt* newspaper office, 1868–1905, this garden store has a TopiGarden in the back that spans two levels. This is one of the gardens on the annual Hermann garden tour. The garden focuses on bird habitats as well as functionality.

Turn right on Fourth Street. Cross Schiller.

6 Gasconade County Historical Society

315 Schiller St.
gasconadecountyhistoricalsociety.com

◆ In October 1969, 75 members of the community came together to form the Gasconade County Historical Society, hosting their first meeting six months later. They wanted to collect and preserve the history of their county before it was lost, and by the end of the year the society was officially recognized as a nonprofit. This stately building is staffed by wonderful volunteers who have a wealth of information to share, and if you have a specific question, they can help you look through the archives. During the days I worked there they were receiving phone calls, emails, and letters from across the country seeking information about relatives in the area. They are also responsible for the designation of historical sites and century homes. They even have a

YouTube channel! Note the statue of George F. Bayer, general manager of the German Settlement Society of Philadelphia's colony, which settled what was hoped to become a city larger than Philadelphia to preserve German heritage, language, and culture.

Return to Schiller. Turn left. Then left (east) on Fourth Street.

7 Old Vine Bed & Breakfast

225 E Fourth St.
oldvinebnb.com

◆ Built for Joseph Rebsamen in 1905, this building is currently an award-winning bed-and-breakfast. The small Queen Anne details make this a distinctive building along the walk.

Courtesy of The Cinema Ship

BONUS WALK

❖ To visit the George F. Bayer gravestone, continue to Gutenberg Street. Turn right and follow the steep hill to the corner of the cemetery. Here you will find Bayer's marker. He was buried on the edge of the cemetery with a decree that no one could be buried within 75 feet of his grave due to the community's dissatisfaction with his performance. For the sesquicentennial, his grave was restored with a stone wall, wrought-iron fence, landscaping, and a bronze plaque. A mock trial was held May 3, 1986, complete with a judge, and Bayer was named as the city's founder.

Enjoy the view from here. You can look over the town and understand why the scouts from the society chose this area to settle.

TOUR THREE

UP THE HILLS: A VOLKSMARCH

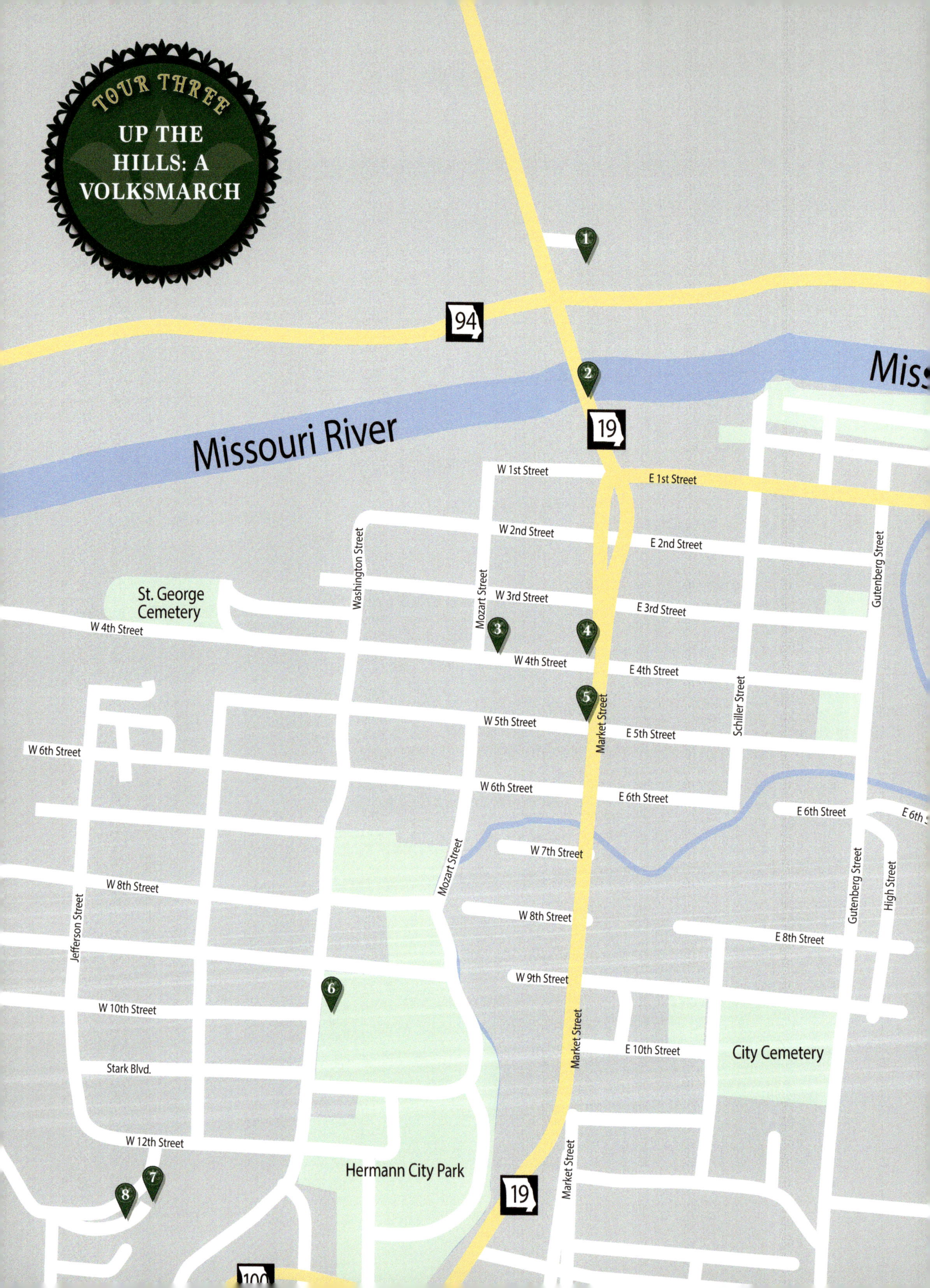

TOUR 3
UP THE HILLS: A VOLKSMARCH

Volksmarch means "people walk." ***Just for fun!*** No competition, no fundraising, just walking for the fun of it with friends and family. It is an organized 5-kilometer (3.1-mile) or 10-kilometer (6.2-mile) walk. I learned about volksmarches when a traveler brought his walking stick on a tour. I asked what all the medals on it represented, and he explained that it showed all the volksmarches he had participated in through the years, providing a commemoration of his time on foot. And he had participated in several in Germany.

This walk has hills and might be more of a *Volkswanderung*, which means "people hike." It is 7.4 miles if you walk up and then back down and 5 miles if you return to Ricky's Chocolate Box. Of course you can choose to drive, too. No one will know! To start, use the address of the Mercantile on the Katy Trail, 500 Walnut Street in McKittrick. It is just off of Missouri Highway 19, which leads south into Hermann. If you are hiking or biking the trail, simply head south on 19 when you arrive at the trailhead.

Courtesy of Flying Squirrel Aerial Optics

1 McKittrick Trailhead
Katy Trail State Park

◆ The Katy Trail is across the river from Hermann on Highway 19 in Montgomery County, and the riders and hikers of the trail often make Hermann an essential stop because of its 300 available rooms and the town's scenery. The trail gives a perspective on the essential need for railroads before roads and rivers were easily traversed. The Katy Trail is the longest railroad line converted into a walking path in the United States. It was an effort the state of Missouri pushed forward for many years, and it finally came to fruition in 1990. It encompasses 240 miles of trail between Clinton and Machens, and users can begin and end at 26 trailheads. For a detailed ride guide, check out Reedy Press author Kathy Schrenk's book *Katy Trail: A Guided Tour through History*.

Courtesy of Flying
Squirrel Aerial Optics

Walk south to the bridge.

2 Senator Christopher S. Bond Bridge

◆ The Christopher S. Bond Bridge opened in 2007. Local resident Florence Mundwiller Kelley was selected to cut the ribbon because she also cut the ribbon for the opening of the original bridge in 1930. That's likely the only bridge in America to make such a claim.

Continue on Market Street and turn right on Fourth Street. This will be a climb.

3 St. George Catholic Church

128 W. Fourth St.
stghermann.diojeffcity.org

◆ Catholicism has always been a part of Hermann. Thirty-three Catholics were among the first wave of settlers, but without a priest they did not have a church of their own and relied on Washington, Missouri, to send one of their Jesuit priests whenever they could, a journey of nearly 30 miles by horse or foot! More than a decade later the Catholics finally built their own church, and in 1849, Fr. Lawrence Kuepfer became the first priest in the newly founded parish of St. George the Martyr. In 1875 the Prussian government forced the Franciscan priests and brothers out of Germany, and many came to the German-speaking parishes throughout the Midwest. Hermann became a retirement facility for Franciscans for many years, which is why the rectory is so large for a relatively small town. With the many Franciscans in Hermann, St. George was able to open a Catholic school in 1879. Construction on the building you see today began in 1915, and soon the church and rectory were completed. The church had a Catholic high school for 20 years, and while it closed in 1970, the elementary school is still going strong under the direction of the laypeople of the church. The church's stained glass windows feature the Corporal and Spiritual Works of Mercy, 14 different ways to care for and love each other.

Come back down to Market Street and reward yourself with the next stop. Turn left on Market Street.

St. George Catholic Church
Courtesy of Flying Squirrel
Aerial Optics

4 Ricky's Chocolate Box

312 Market St.
rickyschocolatebox.com

◆ Craving something sweet? Check out Ricky's Chocolate Box! It is a dream come true for a chocolatier. Ricky Hughey opened the store in 2004, and it continues in his memory today. High-quality handmade chocolates abound, with unique offerings like chocolate chicks filled with jelly beans. Nothing pairs better with wine than chocolate!

Turn right out of Ricky's and continue down Market Street.

5 Sharp Corner Tavern

414 Market St.
facebook.com/SharpCornerTavern

◆ When iron ore was still mined in the surrounding areas, the wagons made a sharp turn onto Market Street, and that sharp turn gave this local gem its name. The name has stuck for nearly 170 years, and the tavern is currently run by Sarah Hoelmer and her son Toby. Sarah's husband, Mitch, passed away in 2019 after running the tavern for 35 years. The tavern is a focal point for the town, and longtime customers who have passed away are memorialized above the jukebox, with their photos, obituaries, and empty bottles of their favorite beverages lined up to honor their memories. Not unlike Cheers, everybody knows your name if you live in town. The menu has remained a standard throughout the years, with traditional bar food that the locals rave about. One in particular is the Herbie Burger: the meat is a specific ratio of meat to fat perfected by Herbie Mueller, the man who owned the tavern before the Hoelmers. Toby picks up the meat daily from Glen Brandt, the butcher in Hermann, so the meat has never been frozen, and it is cooked on a special cast-iron griddle that has been seasoned by years of fantastic burgers. Other specials include the Screwnoodles that Toby's father, Mitch, created—imagine a tasty bar version of Hamburger Helper. The regulars have their seats, most often close to the kitchen so they can chat with the Hoelmers. On the rare occasions that the tavern has to close, Toby can text the regulars. If that's not a slice of life in a small town, I don't know what is.

Courtesy of Michelle Kotthoff

Continue south on Market Street. Turn right on Fifth, left on Mozart, and then wind your way to 11th Street, where you will arrive at your next stop.

6 Rotunda

243 W 11th St.

◆ This was built in 1864 as the Gasconade County Agricultural Association exhibition hall, and the Brush and Palette Club raised the funds and organized the restoration of this fascinating building so it can be used for "virtually any respective purpose including agricultural exhibitions." Their mission: to promote the arts and preserve the culture of the Hermann area.

The Hermann Garden Club is one of the organizations that makes good use of this octagonal location. Not only do they grow flowers, they also tend to the community by using funds raised to support local students through their scholarship program. As you enjoy your walks through town, you are going to see many of the

Courtesy of Flying Squirrel Aerial Optics

wonderful gardens in the area. Many of those are created and tended to by garden club members. Be sure to visit hermanngardentours.com to keep up with all the club's events.

Every Christmas the Gasconade County Historical Society hosts Tablescapes at the Rotunda, a contest where each person entering has a themed table setting for the holidays. The winner is determined by the votes cast by visitors.

And most importantly, the Rotunda is on the National Register of Historic Places, ensuring its ongoing presence in the Upper City Park.

Walk downhill to Eleventh Street. Turn right, then turn left on Washington Street. Turn right on Twelfth Street and turn left on Stone Hill Highway. This is a hearty walk.

7 Stone Hill Winery

1110 Stone Hill Hwy.
stonehillwinery.com

◆ The biggest winery in the Hermann area, Stone Hill has been producing amazing wines since its founding in 1847. Originally known as the Poeschel and Scherer winery, the name changed to Stone Hill once the two owners sold it to their managers,

Courtesy of Declan Rutan

William Herzog and George Stark. Stark became the sole proprietor of Stone Hill in 1893, and soon he developed it into the largest winery west of the Mississippi. With hand-dug caves, they had plenty of space to store wine at the right temperature throughout the year as it aged. Unfortunately, Prohibition destroyed the business, and they turned to growing mushrooms in the cellars to survive. The winery was revived in 1965 when local farmers Jim and Betty Held began to restore the buildings that had been neglected for 40 years. Stone Hill was the first winery to be reestablished in Missouri, and in 1969 the property was listed on the National Register of Historic Places, with 11 buildings associated with the winery included on the list.

Did You Know?

Stone Hill has one of the largest cellars in the world, and at one point it held 1.25 million gallons of wine! One cellar was named **The Vault of the Twelve Apostles** for the 12 large casks that once filled these empty alcoves, each one carved with the likeness of one of the apostles. The carvings were so beautiful that they were a tourist attraction that drew people to Hermann in the 1800s into the 1900s. Employees knew that Prohibition was on the horizon and that these works of art would be destroyed, so they dismantled them and put them on a train hoping to send them to Germany. But World War I was in full swing and the journey proved too difficult. There were German winemakers in South America at the time and the casks may have been sent there for safekeeping, but the destination of the intricately carved casks remains a mystery. The cellars were transformed into mushroom farms until winemaking came back to Hermann in 1965, 30 years after Prohibition was over.

Courtesy of the Library of Congress

❽ Vintage 1847 Restaurant

◆ On the property with Stone Hill, this was formerly a stable. You will notice that the booths are exceptionally long, as they were once the horse stalls.

Courtesy of the Library of Congress

BONUS WALK

As you leave Stone Hill, head west toward 13th Street, continuing onward until you reach Washington Street. Turn right onto Washington for one block, then turn left onto Route 100 and continue over the Frene Creek Bridge. Turn right onto Route 19, turn left onto State Highway H, turn right onto Bavarian Hills Boulevard, and turn left into the plaza. The library is in the building to your right.

The Gallery at the Library

123 Bavarian Hills Plaza A
scenicregional.org/gallery

Located a mile from Stone Hill, this is worth the effort. Although the Hermann library is a modern building, it houses a 2,000-square-foot art gallery, hosting exhibits throughout the year and showcasing regional artists.

Did You Know?

The Wine Trail is not only a path along the road to wineries but also a group of wineries in Hermann that work together to promote special events. Visit hermannwinetrail.com to find out about the events at **Adam Puchta Winery, Dierberg Star Lane Tasting Room, G. Husmann Wine Co., Hermannhof Winery, Reserve Cellars**, and **Robller Vineyard**. They host six events throughout the year focusing on wine and food.

Adam Puchta Winery
Courtesy of Hermann Wine Trail

Chocolate Wine Trail
Fourth weekend of February

Farmers' Table Wine Trail
An early April Saturday

Wild Bacon Wine Trail
First weekend in May

Berries & BarBQ Wine Trail
Last full weekend of July

Holiday Fare Wine Trail
Third weekend of November

Say Cheese Wine Trail
Second Saturday of December

Acknowledgments

I want to express my gratitude to the many people who answered the phone, responded to emails, and spoke to me in person about the history, culture, and tenacity of the citizens of Hermann: Angie Walter at the Gasconade County Historical Society; Corey Orr at Historic Hermann; Tammy Bruckerhoff who wears two hats, one with Visit Hermann and one running her very successful and tasty Sugar Momma's business; Robert Haskins of Visit Hermann who drove me around and directed me to Lois Kruse, a wonderful resource, prolific author, and preservationist of Hermann's history; Elise Bellfontaine for walking and driving me to gardens; Patty Held who has been an amazing resource for years with my tour groups and who is now creating events to bring folks to Hermann; and her nephew Nathan Held who is vigilantly gathering all the historic and accurate information about Stone Hill and the town. His help with the history of the apostle casks was invaluable. And thanks to friend and traveler Bev McMeel for calling on Michelle Kothoff to get those last-minute photos.

Thanks to Maggie Rutherford, our office manager and queen of organization who kept moving our businesses forward when I would spontaneously announce I was hopping on the train to go to Hermann for research. I had peace of mind knowing she was there. And I cannot thank her enough for learning, without hesitation, how to become a booking agent for my book presentations three years ago and handling my individual sales and delivery. She is a friend to the end.

I cannot say enough of the comfort, support, and encouragement from my husband, Declan. His "Hey, how's the Hermann book coming along?" and his help with research and proofreading made a big difference in the final product. I smiled when I read Joe DiGregorio's second book, speaking of Kristin doing the same for him. I miss him. And I miss LynnMarie Alexander, another author who was one of my proofreaders and ardent supporters but most importantly my friend.

This book came out two years later than I intended. We all know where the path of good intentions leads! Declan kept me moving forward with his gentle nudges. That coupled with the one-sentence email from Josh Stevens, founder of Reedy Press, lit a fire under me to finish this project that I had written over and over in my head. Declan is not a native Missourian nor was Jill, my editor, and they posed questions that were clear to me as a Missourian and a tour guide but would be puzzling to someone outside the area. I believe that made this a better book.

Declan is also the one who suggested I dedicate this book solely to Kay Schwinke, who has made both our lives better for knowing her. She is the inspiration for my choice of Hermann as my subject. She constantly kept in touch during the first years of my ownership of Discover St. Louis and showed me the magic in the town. As the most German town in Missouri, Hermann is always a hit for visitors of all ages. And that is because of the people who have stayed for generations since the first settlers and preserved the aim of the German Settlement Society of Philadelphia along with newcomers who admire the success and the culture of the town. My hope is that the mission to preserve German culture continues here for another 188 years.

Sources

Centenarians of Brick, Wood and Stone-Hermann, Missouri by Anna Kemper Hesse

German Settlement Society of Philadelphia and Its Colony, Hermann, Missouri by William G. Bek

Hermann Sesquicentennial by Dorothy H. Shrader

History of Hermann by Samuel F. Harrison

americancountryside.com/2022/04/05/the-twelve-apostles-mystery-in-hermann-missouri

blackshiredistillery.com

city-data.com/picfilesc/picc45653.php

columbiamissourian.com/rivertown/visuals/an-oasis-in-hermann-the-story-of-sharp-corner-tavern/article_66203dec-08c4-11ef-84ac-ffbc3ade600e.html

concerthallandbarrel.com/our-story

cprr.org/museum/gasconade_disaster.html

dannwoellertthefoodetymologist.wordpress.com/2023/07/19/in-search-of-wine-and-norton-grape-pioneer-george-husmann-in-napa-valley

digital.shsmo.org/digital/collection/mhr/id/26014

ecfr.gov/current/title-27/chapter-I/subchapter-A/part-4/subpart-C/section-4.25

en.wikipedia.org/wiki/Gasconade_Bridge_train_disaster

espressolaine.com

evergreenhermann.com

experiencehermann.com/things-to-do/hermann-missouri-services/showboat-community-theatre

extension.iastate.edu/wine/wp-content/uploads/2017/07/winegrowernews260_30dec2013.pdf

fernwehdistilling.com

firehouse.com/operations-training/video/55242075/historic-building-in-hermann-mo-ravaged-by-fire

flickr.com/photos/154988776@N05/52640288556

flickr.com/photos/138779491@N03/53913039373

fourthstreetpizza.com

gasconadecountyhistoricalsociety.com

gasconadecounty.org/about-gasconade-county

gasconadecountyhistoricalsociety.com/you-tube-videos

ghusmannwine.com

greatamericanstations.com/stations/hermann-mo-hem

hermannfarm.org

hermannhof.com

hermannmo.com/rotunda-building

hermannucc.com

hermannwinetrail.com

hermannwursthaus.com

historichermann.com

historichermann.com/167-2

ia801401.us.archive.org/13/items/americangrapegro00husmrich/americangrapegro00husmrich.pdf

innathermannhof.com/about-us

ksdk.com/article/news/local/historic-hermann-building-fire/63-83aab1c5-addd-48db-99a5-46f4dc1747d2

lionheartwhiskey.com

maps.roadtrippers.com/us/hermann-mo/points-of-interest/white-house-hotel

martincitytelegraph.com/2019/12/30/a-gift-to-the-world-of-wine-the-rich-history-of-missouris-vines

missouriwine.org/news/american-viticultural-areas

mms.hermannareachamber.com/hermann/mp_scTheatre#tcs_about_us

mohumanities.org/first-train-first-disaster

mostateparks.com/sites/mostateparks/files/Hermann%20Report.pdf

mostateparks.com/sites/mostateparks/files/Rotunda%2C%20The.pdf

opportunities.ucc.org/CustomerFTP/4990/Attachments/St.%20Paul%20Hermann.pdf

visithermann.com/listing/white-house-hotel-tours

xpps.org/places/the-hofgarten-in-hermann-missouri

ruralmissouri.org/fernweh-distilling-co

scenicregional.org/gallery

solosophie.com/magical-german-travel-words-not-in-english

stghermann.diojeffcity.org

stlmag.com/design/hermann-jim-mary-dierberg-cat-neville

stompngroundsespressobar.com/about-us

stonehillwinery.com/our-story

sugarmommashermannmo.com/about

theclio.com/entry/181821

thewhitehousehotel1868.com

thewohlthouse.com/history.shtml

tinmillbrewery.com

tinmillsteakhouse.com

visithermann.com

waymarking.com/waymarks/wm12YBF_St_Paul_United_Church_of_Christ_celebrates_175_years_Hermann_MO

waymarking.com/waymarks/wm13DP3_Star_Mills_Signage_Gets_Much_Needed_Facelift_Hermann_MO

web.archive.org/web/20080706192819, historycooperative.org/journals/jala/26.1/schwartz.html

web.archive.org/web/20240000000000*, thewhitehousehotel1868.com/history

web.archive.org/web/20240412220705, thewhitehousehotel1868.com/history

Index